AF575579

## PRAISE FOR ~~*PLACE*~~

At once a poetry collection and portal into whole universes of artistic traditions & collectives, ~~*PLACE*~~ gifts us a poetics of organizing our world so desperately needs. "Everything is a question of language," Alexei Perry Cox reminds us, in poems which move, with the patch-working beauty of a cento, across temporalities, languages, and histories. Here is a poet rigorously engaged with the conversations between theory and practice, between intellect and affect, to build beyond the failed imaginations of space our peoples have inherited under colonialism: "we like using graph paper to plot the latitudes and longitudes we can't measure without human inferences." Ambitious in reach, and immense in all the necessary ways, how else could a book so interested in such beyonds end but Return? "I'd made a promise to my mother to go back to the beginning // and I've kept it." I don't remember the last time I was this moved by a collection's convergence towards its final last breath: "I have become more ourselves." Beyond. There are no more words ya اختي.

**—George Abraham**

~~*PLACE*~~ begins from the psychology of ruin, as in, where do we go when the dust lifts and settlers remain, when countries are bombed and people displaced, when arbitrary boundaries have been locked into one's statehood but not one's imagination? Perry Cox speaks to the impossibility of the terrestrial and the territorial: She carries her darlings in her eyeballs, she canoes beyond the edge of an imminent earth, she flees her own consciousness. But even while untethered, she looks back. She dives into the archive and uses transliteration, aphorism, and meta-critical thought experiments to construct her own epistemological groundwork. Here, theory and practice thunder against and with each other. In the end, Perry Cox's most pressing question might be how how does one "uncede" the body? She writes: "Maybe it's too easy to blame mortality on our capacity to love/ the slow death that is putting your breath into another's body." She offers breath where thought fails, and air where the ground no longer is in reach. Perry Cox has a rare cerebral sensibility that is patient with thinking and never opts for an easy catharsis. ~~*PLACE*~~ *illuminates* a poet-philosopher at work, but thank god, also one with blood and heart.

**—Megan Fernandes**

Reading Alexei Perry Cox's ~~*PLACE*~~ for the first time I felt that rarest thing in poetry: the presence of a totally new voice. Or rather, I felt the presence of a totally new chorus of voices—brought together by Perry Cox—singing together in one language, in many languages, in Spanish, Arabic, English, Farsi, French, Mandarin, in joy, terror, history, beauty, physics, family, land. It's a wildly ambitious book, and the miracle is how boldly, capably, it charges into its ambitions, meeting them, often (impossibly!) exceeding them. Perry Cox writes, "All my blood does is run headlong into life;" then she shows us."

**—Kaveh Akbar**

Alexei Perry Cox leans into philosophy, linguistics, history—both recovered and imagined--and geography in an effort to understand herself, to place herself. Ghosts across time and language translate and retranslate themselves into a multi-lingual lyric weave. It's global poetry, sophisticated in thinking and structure and construction but raw and immediate in its import and impact.

**—Kazim Ali**

Cross out "place," and think instead of what sort of poetics may emerge from unceeded, stolen, or lost land. Alexei Perry Cox's new powerful collection is written from a place that isn't one; a site that eludes borders. A diasporic and anti-nationalistic locus that insists on summoning ghosts. Perry Cox dexterously orchestrates multilingual conversations between historical and contemporary figures via citation and translation—two inherently relational practices. Revolutionary archives are re-organized into formally intricate poems, reminding us that "… embracing a newfound freedom is embracing the freedom to imagine it" (Rinaldo Walcott cited by Alexei Perry Cox). What results is an associative and at times dreamlike linguistic terrain capacious enough to hold the trying nature of revolutionary hope. In the company of so many, Alexei invites us to join an assembly in which imagining another form of citizenry together is momentarily possible.

**—Mirene Arsanios**

What if everything that has been said is being said again with everything and everyone in mind? What if, after accepting that simple was never a reality, reality becomes something we won't simply accept? What if at the centre of the universe there really is a woman, some seeds, and revolution? A poem can live in the body until an abrasion, a rupture, lets it leak like a vapor in the air before you, something like a door you never knew you were lacking, and which calls you on...I think that's what Alexei Perry Cox is after in these poems.

**—Sina Queryas**

Alexei Perry Cox utilizes incredible rational and philosophical stances in her work which point to her being a notable thinker. The main energies in the text involve time, the passage of time, the inability to come to terms with a constantly shifting time and also a shifting geography. In other words, Perry Cox's work embraces the concept of universal *flux*.

> Because the scalpel of intellect isn't able to adequately discern between operation and autopsy, the object of its incision is abstract at first and only during the act itself does it emerge from the fog of unconsciousness into the sphere of understanding to gradually acquire the face of a conscious reality.

With Arabic and other contemporary intertextuality, Perry Cox underscores that "some of the things we try to understand are simply incomprehensible, and this is precisely because of their essence;" and asks questions like: "Why do we so stubbornly look for locks to every door—even the ones that are already open?" Cox also engages in the book with notions of hyper-masculinity and the female condition, with the concluding pages being more focused on mothers and motherhood.

**—E. Zisimatos**

# ~~PLACE~~

# ~~PLACE~~

ALEXEI PERRY COX

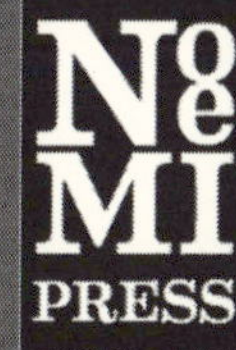

Published By Noemi Press, Inc. A Nonprofit Literary Organization. www.noemipress.org

Cover Art by Marie-Douce St-Jacques
Cover Design by Maya Moumne
Book Design by co•im•press
Arabic Proofreadiing by Raja Salim

ISBN: 978-1-934819-47-0

*for you:*
*the future revolves around you and your future revolutions*
*and our paradoxes of emancipation*

## On Method

Je voudrais sans la nommer / vous parler d'elle.
—Georges Moustaki

If the site of investigation is a poetics of organizing rather than unearthing an archive or banging a drum, the question of theory and practice is thought concomitantly with the dialectic of revolutionary hope and political disenchantment:

One was dealing with oneself as if under a constant demand, as an employee of history or steward of the future, with many tasks to achieve; this is the organization.

How to be a scribe to a vanishing world, one comes to terms with one's inheritance; as one always has.

Hard to shake off one's own assassination, too. Hard to be memorable, hard to be militant, hard to be generous with time and suggestions.

I learned so much from burning about how to be characteristically off-the-cuff, which burns too.

## Contents

*I am writing with my burnt hand about the nature of fire.*
—Ingeborg Bachmann (tr. Philip Boehm)

*Anybody who thinks that they can understand how terrible the terror has been,*
*without understanding how beautiful the beauty has been against the*
*grain of the terror, is wrong.*
—Fred Moten

# Home

# Exile

## My grandmother remembers "A Criticism of [Im]pure Reason" as song

*Abuela* sings. She sings on the terrace of the house with the shutters
where her father will be assassinated.

*Un día mi cabello será blanco*[1], she sings, when she is only a daughter still.
Her heart full of health, cheeks full, lungs warm.

Her hair white, she tells me: I can never cry all the tears in my body
since his death, *entiendes*?

*Abuela* sings. In the sky of Matanzas a gigantic balloon full of green spiders
passes by like *un pavo real blanco pasa.*[2]

*Abre la puerta de su casa y entra /como un desconocido*, she sings in aeolian,
*como si penetrara en el mundo / por la puerta de atrás.*

Open the door of your house and enter / as a stranger,
as if it penetrated by the world / by the back door.[3]

The house with the shutters will long remember the bomb that cracked the façade
where later she'll put plastic flowers.

---

[1] *Un día mi cabello será blanco tr.* One day my hair will be white. (from "Crítica a la razón impure")

[2] *Un pavo real blanco pasa* tr. A white peacock passes by. (a line from Rubén Darío used by revolutionaries to forewarn of danger)

[3] translated lines of the preceding stanza (from "Crítica a la razón impure")

## My home and native (unceded) body

I guess you can say my mother had a type: haunted men / dead men /
men marked to die.

I guess you can say my mother was a type: haunted woman / dead woman /
woman marked to die.

Maybe it is too easy to blame mortality on our capacity for love:
the slow death that is putting your breath in another's body.

After all without my not-yet mother's nutmeg calves finding love for the night
I could not have been born.

My adoption papers mark me equally *Odanak Abenaki* and blue-eyed and taken
because *back home no place for a blonde baby, bush lady*.[4]

I guess you can say my body, like the land, was up for grabs:[5] *kwai kwai,*
*Niwaskowôgan, can you take me instead?*[6]

I guess you can say my body had a blood type: haunted / dead /
marked to die.

---

[4] lyric from Alanis Obomsawin's song "Bush Lady" about children of mixed heritage being taken from the Abenaki reserve

[5] reference to a line by Billy-Ray Belcourt (from "Boyfriend Poems")

[6] *kwai kwai Niwaskowôgan* tr. Welcome, Great Spirit.

## Our (un)atlas colouring book

We begin because the world before ours ended and what is this country
    but the drawing of a line.

I draw thick black lines around my eyes and they are a country
    by what belongs to me.

When we, you and I, talk about geography I ask if you think a nation is made
    by its founding fathers.

Let oceans close back up my eyes when you respond with your father tongue
    我们要学的事情挺多.[7]

I have learned that my love of you has made me not want to die in this nation
    and you teach me 就睁开了一只眼睛.[8]

Wind to the sails on the night sea while you are sleeping like the child you are
    and I know I will be murdered by your father.

I leave a final note on your drawing table: *Everywhere is a foreign land.*
    *In death finally there is no home to try to go back to.*[9]



---

[7] 我们要学的事情挺多 tr. We still have so much to learn. (from Gu Gong poem "人儿" or "Little People" tr. Li Xia

[8] 就睁开了一只眼睛. tr. I open wide an eye. (from Gu Gong's poem "杨树" or "Poplar" tr. Joseph R. Allen)

[9] Translated from a letter by Xie Ye to their son Sam

## My [your] home movie

Of the films you never made during *les années des plomb*[10]
    my favourite is *Territoire de L'instant* (*Land of the Moment*).

After your funeral, I use the video camera you used to document my dance recitals
    to film a horizon cracked in two.

The opening scene is so revealing that I ask Emma Ramadan
    to translate the *sous-titres* from your Arabic to my French to English:

*My blue sky between two eclipses of swallows tells of war all the tall volcanoes of long ago.*
    *In the lava recklessly we forged fantastic lives in which we weren't prisoners.*[11]



In the film underneath my film of your film, I am a tap dance unleashed
    and you can be heard to laugh with your wife my mother [off-screen].

The act of my eclipse becomes the source
    of the imaginative act of your regeneration.

وساءلتني عن غيابي كلما واجهته واجهت معنىً للغياب you tell me[12]
    as if for a moment, an instant, the land can bend and open up you to me.

---

[10] *les années des plomb* tr. The Years of Lead

[11] Emma Ramadan's translation from Ahmed Bouanani's *Photograms*

[12] وساءلتني عن غيابي كلما واجهته واجهت معنىً للغياب tr. Whenever I face it, I face a new meaning for absence (from Touda Bouanani's collection of her father's unpublished script for *Territoire de L'instant*)

## In a vice grip with my lover (in exile)

As time went by, an urgent desire overtook my lover
gradually made as futile as the world spinning:

A desire to grasp the secret of the present,
and see a system's undulating veil.

In the universe of our civil war,[13] systems
had the insubstantiality of hummingbird's song.

The iridescence of its plumage
while their manifestations were immutable.

Told that my love for my lover was a vice,
that loving another woman wasn't womanly of me

that *our* civil war as being "against ourselves,"
wasn't the same as *their* civil war being against us.

My lover believed there had to be a point at which reality
would get through to humankind.

---

[13] The Lebanese Civil War 1975-1990

In exile in Paris and Sausalito, *I want you to touch me here and here. I want it to be warm for me for you.*
*I want to love systems that are woman so that you can enter them by being one too.*

"Vice," my lover said between each sigh, "has no limits. And there are so many vices!
The less I understand how life can suffice to give an idea of how many vices there are!"

for Etel Adnan

## The balcony of Hazama Habayeb collapses

*Utillu ka shurfati baytin 'ala ma 'urid* transliterates Darwish: *Like a house's balcony,*
*I overlook what I desire*[14]

The world is exposed in an explicit way
over and over at the closest furthest distance of the self
to the sort of things she had always been thinking at around that time:

Likewise worried about wars and translations as much as dinner,
when it happens she reminds the nation's children that pick her up:
*If I die, leave the balcony open (Si muero dejad el balcón abierto*[15]*)*

Her laughter seems like a solitary echo swallowed up by a vast desert
increasingly more peopled by the vastness that has taken place.
It has a mystical edge when she asks: Can one die doing what one does best

if what one does best is

"suspend thought"?



[14] Hazama Habayeb's transliteration of Mahmoud Darwish's "I see my ghost coming from afar"
[15] Federico Lorca's "Farewell" (translated by W.S. Merwin)

میهن من

In a museum park in the middle of Tehran, a family of peacocks
walks about freely.

One of the park visitors opens a bag of birdseed
and disturbs the majesty of the much-admired father peacock.

Shahin, my friend, has been writing a screenplay in exile
using the words of, amongst others, Sohrab Sepehri.

SOHRAB

The relationship between me
and my environment was mostly a fragile one.
In Tehran when I sat in my writing room
a panic would grab my confidence and run out the door.
To where? Is anywhere the right place?
A place that only belongs to me
is a false expectation. One should be able
to write poetry on park benches.

In the margins, I write "And what of the much-overlooked mother peahen?
Could she resemble Forough Farrokhzad?"

As one who, keeping still, can suggest translated lines such as
"This is a map drawn from memory of the specular itinerary of exile."

میهن من is "My homeland" in Farsi
for Shahin Parhami

## በስራ ላይ

Ghassan's mother said, "I thought for a time if we died we might escape
the sovereignty of the accidental."

When she showed up in Dakar with a huge suitcase, she was there
by accident.

The burning heat in her eyes was also in her belly – it contrasted
the displacement that marked her personality.

Her smallish figure was in stark opposition to the size of her luggage
but silently this, too, was being changed.

She sat on L'Indépendance park bench until the pregnancy was too hot
to sit in the heat.

Later, Ghassan asked his mother what it meant to become his mother
in exile:
"I learned that Amadou Bamba theorized that all babies are a
welcome accident."

በስራ ላይ is "Memory Country" in Wolof

## ငါ၏အစာတိမြေ

I am in the groove made by a golf car wheel in The People's Square
and Park in Yangon.

In the erasure of the destruction left intact for the insatiable
cameras of untalented visitors to collect.

You tell me what ရန် (*yan*) and ကုန် (*koun*) mean respectively: "enemies"
and "run out of."

On the landing you stood proud amongst ghosts, as if the colonists
were translucent behind us.

A guy with three mobile phones held like three hard cocks reacts to a remark
you make in English:

"This place is playing chess with us." The guy enacts a gunslinger, pointed smile
as if to say *You're lucky because right now we're all just having a good time here.*

ငါ၏အစာတိမြေ is "My homeland" in Burmese

*Organisation is the form of mediation between theory and practice.*
—Georg Lukács (tr. Rodney Livingstone)

# Auditorium

# Moratorium

## *Of Metrical Composition*

*——yes,*
*an almost impenetrable natural barrier*
*that's what all the historians and travelers said*
*yet*

at the same time, one could follow
another invented, winding direction
marked by a bold dashed line
as an upward path on the ribs of the atlas
excavating those inaccessible lands——

*that's that*
the versification professor says
——a heavy-set man——
takes off his jacket
rolls up his sleeves
lights up a cigar

his squint eye
switches from presence to absence
with the drive of someone in a continuous monologue
with himself——

*I think that . . . we . . .*
tries to visualize the words,
puffs out smoke,
clears his throat
*we can't not be part of . . . the movement*——



*waqifuuhum innahum mas'uuluun*

The laser spot appears
disappears flickers
leaps from place to place
skips
beams in short
quick blinks
returns to its point of departure

suddenly calms down
almost sweeps across the illuminated surface
to the right
where it rests
the tip of the long
thin plastic pointer stops for a second
quivers in the dust that slowly turns into a half-shadow
then caught by a sudden fever –
a growing dancing tongue of flame –
it blazes from one side of the map to the other
withdraws all at once
then moves forward again as if exploring a border
it seems that it disappears
but it reappears
flies like an arsonist setting fire to a field
or like erupting gunfire
explores the void
the shadow
or more precisely –
the light layer of the shadow;

The woman stands at the podium plays
with the pointing stick with one hand, leans
against the table with the other, rests her body, her torso
outlined in the half-dark, her widely opened collar shows
yellow alabaster skin where soon a bead of sweat
will appear, the muscles of her neck and throat,
taut with tension, strain then relax, reach up
to the restless chin and its complex working machine;
"Here. This is one of the ways things are done differently
in Poetry From the Arab World."
A kind of subtlety in its sharpness, it bends the medium,
exposes the sullen, hermetic amphitheater to something
jolting, something disturbing for a moment; but without
lessening its vehemence, it suddenly stops; an unexpected
caesura, while the echo still reverberates in the distance;

*waqifuuhum innahum mas'uuluun*
*tr. But stop them, for they must be asked*

## 百姓

We were required to follow the analysis
for several years, one or two hours per week:
happiness,
creation and its forms – thought and space
the happiness, *hic et nunc*, that which every
Westerner also will refer to
We, the scholars, sat in the dark cell partly
illuminated by the light coming from the
narrow window
Our head bowed, thoughtful,
while the winding staircase next to us spiraled
up, as we continued our meditation

the screen would turn
into a mental stage that widened
as we learned how to connect,
move beyond axioms, piece together
evidence, prove conclusions,

enter another world
completely different from the one that we had
entered when we heard,    for the first time
*the East is red* in the labyrinth *siheyuan* of
Beijing

牌

and there was still the end of history, after
which everything returned to the beginning, a
kind of recorded fairy tale, which every living
person would read – and the events?



They were more or less colourful incidents
colouring it with contemporary hues
a system of sound traversing through the city
—an endless, continuous process that had its
          own course and that had undergone a gradual
inflection, a thesis, an antithesis
          repeated in the previous
    century, then again by the many of us, had

drowned already; as we were collecting
our papers, the unopened books that we had
produced from our worn satchels, rare, heavy
books that made an impression, as would a
          hermetic sentence made collective

as soon as the noise erupted, the almost
invisible door
at the front, to the right
would open and the custodian in his white
coat would appear
              白日依山尽
              黄河入海流
   white sun against mountain leans
       yellow river into sea flows
The world is not "world" but "the earthly"
(天下, literally "under the sky"). One seldom
hears people talk about "citizens" in China
because we are "hundreds of names" (百姓).

*百姓 tr. *hundreds of names*

### ***As noted: Language Is Migrant***

I had written down

The

surprising evolution of the Spanish word *querer*
reflects very well the nature of this quest; *querer*
comes from the Latin *quarere* (to search, to inquire),
but in Spanish the meaning soon changed, and
the word came to mean *desire, to love.*     *Querer*
: a passionate, amorous quest.     A quest
whose goal lies neither in the future nor in the past,
but at that point of convergence that is
the beginning and the end
: the time before the beginning and after the end.



I was beside
the dynamic young woman next to me
who was either busier with her notes

When Cecilia Vicuña describes her experience of asking passersby
the repeated question of "What is poetry to you?"

while in exile in Bogotá in 1980
she reveals that her favourite answer was "Que prosiga,"
"That it may go on."

or would occasionally glance up
from beneath her eyelashes
as if somewhat indifferent
while her loose hair
and armpits diffused in the air
con*quering*

### *Act One or One Act:*

Aleppo, 1979

It had taken us out of ourselves, changed

In a foreigned language, ثورة made sense to us
when the speaker
asked us to *Act it out*

we could all head to another place just like this one
    but slightly different



and so were making loud decisions
as we said It

    [ the banging fist,

        *. . . by the Ministry of Education . . .*
        ineffectively, the Chair
            calling for order

    the same banging again ]

the revolution was dislodging stones
passions were spilling over
blossoming:

one word putting an end to the chewing
of watered-down words

*ثورة tr. *change or revolution*

## ثورة

Beirut 1982

on It
captivated we clapped and smoked
spellbound by the new word that belonged to no one
to no one side!
you got up from your seat, stood up and it was
yours for a second
the second you said it
and we, like strikers, were the actors of history who
were called to change life
with It

[ the Chair was now inviting
the last presenter of the
panel,
whose works were familiar to
everyone ]

weighing It
as it were, what was time?
he held the watch in his palm, it was gold, no, it was nothing!
nothing but sand, nonexistence, and there were
things that never passed
things that were eternal, everlasting, he scratched
his beard
still protected from the semidarkness
smoothed It

*so . . . you are this panel's last*
*presenter*
[ gesturing with his

right hand—]

*shall we start?*

## *[ Following a Tough Act ]*

Paris 1968

*Ce n'est pas facile*
his voice
a sudden rise, now he tries to make a joke
as if it were necessary
to bring some sort of merriment to the atmosphere
*It's a tough act to follow this: I would like to,*
*comment dit-on, change the . . . direction*

[ effectively making use

of the staged directions ]

*Alors*
*let me remind you all: one has to maintain the seriousness*
*the circumstances of the material and place, avoiding*
*at the same time the boredom that such materials,*
*such analyses might cause, proceeding as traditional*
*narratives do, long winding, weaving into each other, as*
*if the same mood had been recurring in different forms*
*and voices from the beginning of civilization*

[ laughter erupts, interrupts ]

exhausted, crumpled, reforming sentence

*L'imagination prend le pouvoir. Bon, Allons-y . . .*
*Mais . . . Ce n'est pas la premi*ère *fois. That is all I am*
*saying. Remember: it was hung in the square. Art is dead,*
*ideas are dead, and death is counter-revolutionary.*
*Really, why should one die? Idiots. Keep walking, non?*

[ mass exodus ]

* *L'imagination prend le pouvoir* —Pierre Alechinsky
(tr. Stedelijk Musem) *Imagination seizes power*

[

we then descended, hung on to the other
the noise, the laughter, the slogan of the day
rose from the front rows, beamed, split into factions
like pigeons excreting on everything
bounced off the screens, to the streets, to the square

—tying a tie, fixing a *keffiyeh*, rolling a cigarette—

the us rumbled, thundered
the coils of smoke
everywhere, ascended, infiltrated
the air a thick misty dome
while the Chair, purpled, raged – as reported in the
press— tried to institute silence, so his colleagues
could speak
one of them had Mao's *Little Red Book* in his hand
another held Lenin's tract: *put an END to civilization!*
*SOON, SOON, the flames will materialize THE*

*FUTURE!*
and another with Camus earmarked at *Every act of rebellion expresses a nostalgia for innocence and an appeal to the essence of being*

and we wanted to live, we wanted to unlearn everything that we had learned, the green or red or blue or black night, while the mezzanine gradually emptied out, everyone descended from the top rows joined people in the front, coughed, wanted to speak, to piss, the hall soon empty and the square too
the footsteps died out, dust, the smell of cigarettes soon everything in ruins, and so everything is a question of language

]

*There are two ways of making investigations, one is to look at flowers on horseback and the other is to get off your horse and look at them.*

**—Mao Tse-tung (tr. Foreign Languages Press)**

***To tell stories***

An austere and coldhearted woman she was
to never smile.

Had the hardness of her heart spread
to her womb

Turned
to stony ground

In which no seed could take
to root

Or had her heart turned
to stone from grief over the absence of offspring?

Amina wondered as she stood before the fire
to flatten the loaves.



«أخبرني القصة، قمر»
"Tell me the story, Qamar."

Qamar used to hide lumps of sugar in his pocket
to give to the children.

Qamar –
cut off like a tree limb, fatherless, motherless, wifeless, childless –
and, yet for all that,
to spread as the branches of jasmine spreads

Over the walls of the houses
to tell the children his stories.

Amina remembered what it was like
to be a child.



«أخبرني القصة، قمر»
"Tell me the story, Qamar."

The story of the frog who married two gazelles.
The story of the box in which the tarantula collected stars.
The story of the sun and the moon.

Qamar told her the story
to make Amina quiet.

Amina clutched the hem of his *jilbaab*
to keep him from leaving her.

"I must return
to my palace, Amina."

"I'll let you go if you promise
to tell me another story."

«احكي القصة، أمينة»
"You tell the story, Amina."



"The absence of children
to harden a heart

Or the hardening of a child
to make a womb a stone,"

Murmured Amina as she tended
to her baking.

*To wait for the news*

Amina is afraid of the sea,
to her mind she pretends otherwise:

to begin before the rooster
to come before the tide comes
to the beach
to the port and inquires,

"Any news?"



"No news."

بِسْمِ اللهِ الرَّحْمٰنِ الرَّحِيْمِ

to the hill
to the high house
to the women's quarters
to the process of sifting,

"Any news?"

"No news."

بِسْمِ اللهِ الرَّحْمٰنِ الرَّحِيْمِ

to afternoon prayer
to her dress and headscarf
to whisper another prayer
to the port again and inquires,

"Any news?"

"No news."

بِسْمِ اللهِ الرَّحْمٰنِ الرَّحِيْمِ

to go to sea:

to go and come back
to go and not come back
to wait for them
to wait for news of them,

“Any news?”

“No news.”

بِسْمِ اللهِ الرَّحْمٰنِ الرَّحِيْمِ

*

Umm Latif did not bear
to wait any longer:

to hear what she had heard
to announce in a voice she tried
to keep to a whisper
to ring like a bell,

“Tomorrow the queen of the English

language is coming to the island.”

*bismillah-alrahman-alrahim*

Amina is afraid to foresee,
that the sea is generous:

to know for certain
to rend garments
to wail with cries that split the air
to cleave it in two as the executioner's blade cleaves

the living head

from the body.

*In the name of God, most Gracious, most Compassionate*

***From Diaspora to My Unborn Island***

I grew and    /    /    /    /
/    /    /    my rift grew
Inside of    it:    /    you live    before
belonging    /    you belong    to no one    country [same]
you belong    to no one    language    /    [*revisa mi lengua*[16]]
you belong    to no one    in the way    you have    never left me
I thought I'd    be older    before    starting    to ask
what if I    die    what happens    to everything    you haven't
yet    /    /    /    said
look    I'm    a sad girl    from    a long line    of sad girls
doesn't mean    I can talk    /    to you    that way
you understand / my problem
you are inside me and your eyes are my darlings
they make me forget the living still beside/s me

16 *revisa mi lengua* = check my tongue

## *From a certain logic for dis/appearing*

> *You cannot live the same life as you imagine. You must live a smaller life, a more compact life. The life you imagine is too capacious, you will lose your balance. Driving home, I think this.*
>
> from "VERSO 24" *The Blue Clerk,* Dionne Brand

A door opens on an eye
the eye opens on a line
the line of eyes looking into a coffin
carrying the body to the river
and into a vision.
You know your conscience cannot forgive
what left you long ago: washed away by summer floods
like a human body loosened from a grip
into something death made transformative:
You cannot live the same life as you imagine. You must live.

There is a word
the word never makes
it breaks against
the inner walls of one's teeth
until it flattens into fizz.
The word is as the moon's eclipse is
the distance between my eye and my hand as a highway
with no hope of ever reaching its end or where I begin
to celebrate the choice that answers my life like a quiz:
a smaller life, a more compact life. The life you imagine is.

Only the dead are alive
nowadays anyways
even as a new you moves about the womb
like he moved about the country like a sword
or like a bull dog in a china room.
Your world is smaller than the center of your eye
but my eye opens the page to a new line:
The "I" is the miracle of the "You" I divine.
This insignificant interval between a death and to die:
too capacious, you will lose your balance. Driving home, I.

A book without room
for the world would be
no book.
It would lack the most beautiful pages (the ones left)
in which even the smallest pebble is reflect.
The present is the time of writing, both obsessed with
and cut-off from an out-of-time brimming with life:
Fabulous a wing unfolding in the paltry field of things
while night finds no consolation in night but in its eclipse:
think this.

*Le désespoir est une forme supérieure de la critique.*

**—Léo Ferré**

## Public

Private

**The people want to fall, the people want the fall**

سَبّح باسم الله[17]
There is no "people."

It is a mistake to focus excessively
on the specifics.

كافر [18]
I am not pan-Arab
and I am not embarrassed.

One is struck by ubiquity
wherever Arabic is spoken.

أخي [19]
I will sail past the shorelines of the two seas of my unrest
through the nations of my neighbors
to rest my conscience in your lands.

The greatest sower of unrest in the region
is neighbor against neighbor.

I did not sail,[20] روحي
Your people took my unstamped passport,
stopped me at the passing.

---

[17] *I praise your name Allah*, [incredulously]
[18] *Infidel* or *Unbeliever*, [incitefully]
[19] *My brother*, [without love]
[20] *My soul*, [without soul]

*My* people?
My people wouldn't do such a thing.
There is no people.

### *A Place for Change* ثورة *(or Revolution)*

Rights + Principles
حقوق + مبادئ

Is that a right (or dream)? أذلكَ حُلْمٌ؟
Torn apart by doubt in confusion and darkness تمزِّقُهُ مُدْيةُ الشكِّ في حَيْرةٍ وظلامْ
What about the genius of the moon hiding then appearing? عن القَمَر العبقريّ أتاهَ وراءَ الغمامْ؟
Illuminated in flicker the way to every distant right decision (or dream) يضيءُ الطريقَ إلى كلّ حُلْمٍ بعيدِ القَرَارْ
The principle (or wish) to appear and disappear تبدو أن تبدو وتختفي
To reveal a place for change (or revolution) ثورة[21]



[21] حقوق renders into English as either rights or dreams
مبادئ renders into English as either principles or wishing
ثورة renders into English as either change or revolution

### *Measures of Historia*

AA: You need to fix the world in some way
*necesita arreglar el mundo de algún modo*
as if everything was measurable.

VE: I was surprised my new body
was more necessary than the woman
trying to measure it to the man measured.

AA: I look at your face *como un desconocido*
as a stranger before our fingers begin
the work of love as a futile crime.

VE: I was surprised as a woman
when he didn't lie to me
*como si estuviera delante de un jurado* as if in front of a jury.

AA: Perhaps a mouth begins to open
then closes on your left breast
where the bullet spoke its one clipped syllable.

VE: I was surprised my body fit so cleanly
into the sea *en las paredes navega el barco*
on the waves of ships the sails.

AA: I watch you die too early to see
what you have done *arreglar el mundo de algún modo*
to fix the world in some way.

VE: I was surprised I was him looking at the ocean. Inside the head I've placed above his torso, one thought turns
over and over and won't go away, the wave curling indifferently a precise distance from the gun on the table
a ruler carved into its surface, inch by inch, as if everything was measurable: death, time, intent, *excepto amor.*[22]



[22] tr. *with the exception of love*

[*Night 3*] [ اليوم ٣ ]

The narration washes up there where you unravel, هنا فوقَ هذا المكانُ تموتُ الجهاتْ. تموتُ الجهاتْ
the autobiographical account is an imposture, ونزوعٌ شحيحٌ إلى رجْفة للشتاء الذي أطفأتْني أكاذيبُهُ
(as if you didn't know that already): you are unable—هنا فوق هذا المكانُ تعلّمتُ معنى السقوط
—to unwind the nonexistent spool of a film that was never shot, وجلستُ أُقاسي افتقاراً إلى الوهم
fragments of moments superimpose each other, cancel each other out, رأيْتُ المَشاهدَ تهْوي
there are only erasures, in your memory, everything has dispersed, لا أصدِّقُ مِمّا أرى غيرَ يأسي
under the spectrum of what became of you: هنا فوق هذا المكانِ الذي يكْفَهِرُّ
could you even render a cubist portrait, أراهُ هنا وهنالك، أصفرَ، مِلءَ الشوارعِ
an allusive portrait, a portrait in fragments, فوق هذا المكان الذي يكْفَهِرُّ كوجه الطَّريدةْ
no, not even. Indecipherable, بعدما خلّفتْني على شرفة من ظلال المغيب وحيداً

what machine, what fiction must you invent, كلماتٌ، رأيتُها تعبُرُ السهْلَ سريعاً، فيستفيقُ الفضاءُ
or construct to manage to capture, كلماتٌ، تَمرُّ بالشجرِ الواهي مروراً، فيعتريه البكاءُ
what would only be an abstract figure, هي البلادُ، التي ضاعتْ، ونحن الفلولُ والأشلاءُ
a figure pierced with ellipses, يا بلاداً، أمستْ بنا مُقفِراتٍ، وغَدَوْنا، فما هناك نَجاءُ
and the enigma that you become, يا بلاداً، نقولُها ونُسمّيها، فتبكي الأقوالُ والأسماءُ
in the space and light of memory, تدوخُ في الزمنِ الرَّخْو، وتُودي بسمْعِها الأصداءُ
you struggle with this impossible memory, كيف أضحى الزمانُ فينا قليلاً؟
you cannot recount. Tenderness devastates you, تزْدرينا ظلالُهُ الصفراءُ
and here is the core of your powerlessness: ليس إلا الذهولُ، في كلِّ صوْبٍ
you had more desire. And when it comes to that, وإذ سِرْتَ، فالدروبُ رياءُ

there is no way you can resort to the half-ironic, كلماتٌ، نُقيمُ فيها
half-moral perspective that allows for that narration, إذا عزَّ مقَامٌ، وأطبَقَتْ أرجاءُ
this aloof point of view that outlines and pins down, كلماتً، هي الديارُ
that immobilizes the memory under the lamp, هي الأرضُ لنا، والسماءُ
or under the tongue, and, methodically, like a scalpel, والأشياءُ
observes and describes it. Autopsy. A cold narration, لا شيءَ ينهضُ
consistent with desire. You cannot recount, . . . حتى الكلامْ
and the reason is visible in the traces that remain, هنا ترقص التُّرَّهاتْ
in that partially electric haunt of phosphorescent signals, ساءلتني عن غيابي
that you rifle through dust, in search of clues, كلما واجهته واجهت معنىً للغياب
as to the genesis, forgotten like all the rest, ما أقصرَ الحياة
of a word that you conceived of at that time. وما أطولَ يومي هذا

The instant and memory

*Acute Dialectic*

Definition of beauty:
Articulation
Makes its limits known to me

*

我所渴望 的美，是永恒与生命
生命的美，千变万化，
却终为灰烬[23]

Movement and immobility

*Poiesis:*

Makes indeterminacy
Visibility
Of vanished overshadows

*

*Ah, I see now,*
*I must first reject*
*my own bargains with the wall*
*to battle my fears out in the world.*[24]

Contingency and Circumstance

*Over and over*

A woman and a dog roll
She is indistinct
But every hair curling

*

*You are a little dog*
*often groaning at the door*
*of my conscience.*

*Tonight, in the long silence*
*again I am thinking of you.*[25]

[23] In "美" ("Beauty"), Gu Cheng writes: "The beauty I thirst for is perpetual if compared to life; [...] the beauty of life, is constantly changing, / but in the end it becomes ashes" (tr. Anna Simona Margarito)

[24] from Shu Ting's "墙" ("The Wall") (tr. Gordon T. Osing & De-An Wu Swihart)

[25] from Ha Jin's translation of her own poem "Again, These Days I Have Been Thinking of You"

Pathos

*Hours*

What night will open
Onto our prisons with stars
Dies the morning light

*

难道飞翔的灵魂
将终身临禁在自由的门槛[26]

Perception

*Over*

At the horizon
Children are carried away
Across the threshold

*

不要哭了，孩子，
当你有一天想变成为：
一朵云、[27]

Affect, Emotion

*Lasts*

Blood still pools a death
Its silence hides it out loud
In the red gutters

*

仿佛 永远分离
却又终身相依
这才是伟大的爱 情
坚贞就在这里
也爱你的坚持的位置[28]



26 In "船" ("Boat"), Shu Ting writes: "Will the fluttering soul / Really be imprisoned forever on the threshold of freedom" (tr. Daniela Zhang-Cziráková

27 In "致大海" ("To the Ocean"), Shu Ting writes: "Don't cry, my child / But one day, when you will want to change into: / a cloud" (tr. Daniela Zhang-Cziráková)

28 In "致橡树" ("To an Oak"), Shu Ting writes: "We may seem forever severed / But are life-long companions. / This is the greatest of love; / This is constancy: / […] I also love also the ground you hold" (tr. Eva Hung)

*What gets from the territory onto the map?*

**—Gregory Bateson**

MATTERS

## Matters

**Wherever one lives on this planet it's ridiculous to try to escape.**

I refer only to matters that make up certain more subtle forms of logic, which deconstruct ourselves through concrete actions against our bodies, or our souls, which are our lands. I'm speaking about the fissures through which we've come to understand what's at stake inside me too, and you, and what's lying in wait for us.

at stake / land matters / unceded / unseeded.

The fissures of this hellish geometry, with virulent blisters, whose pain has already metastasized: they say they'll give compensation later in another language.

**It wasn't only that the intensity of light and space shrank that shrank.**

The buildings of their theories keep falling down and from the other side of the façades, the whole has revealed to me, with greater force, the reach of my unreality and the fissure of the symbolic. We have to unmake our reality under the influence of other scenes and a different syntax. Maybe we have to remake them with the simplest thing: with what remains and with the remainder of ourselves.

capacity to survive / capacity to act



During the first fifteen days, time dilated— it seemed that lengthy years must have passed—as if it had drained off toward the narrowest section of the tunnel, or better said, the pipeline through our lifelines.

**Everyone oppresses the space you have for memories.**

And the space becomes a region in colour, a mental space I kept trying to possess while simultaneously surrendering impossible things. The anguish came with little details of survival—the way urgency is rustic—and the dynamics of my freedom as our freedom shrank to a minimum. As if the return were occurring in a different time, with a different velocity.

they observe it / then destroy it

I had crossed over with the attitude and the latitude that they wouldn't take it away from me. I could clearly see the waste from futile events, as we misused pleasure. We made commentaries and gestures against the inertia and disillusionment and apathy of our times. The greatest disaster wasn't merely psychological but was psychological.

**Awareness grew like the vertigo from their rhetoric.**

My friends (the most intelligent ones) had wagered their lives on the land under observation through a vulgar microscope, where they made minimal evolutions and revolutions in their capacity to survive. The zones of possibility were getting blocked or cut off before any birth – or victory – in place of reason they substituted certain logics for getting through the short term at all costs; the easiest route was escape, indifference.

fight / flight / right / rights



Then, sordid traces of personality and ego appear, strengthened in the fight to get to a place that doesn't exist for them, one they have no right to get to.

**The speed with which we assemble things destroys reality.**

At that point I had to adapt as if it were something normal, though acquired in circumstances of not being normal, like other subterfuges that drained my energy. I hadn't only lost the center, but the vision – the one that used to allow me to find relations from a certain distance with intervals of deep understanding, the flame.

constituted / measured / elemental comparison

What have we done with our existence: it's understanding that a cerebration has been produced for which there is no aesthetic place.

**There is still no aesthetic which could relate the thing conceived to its immediate materialization.**

That lack of coordination extends the feeling of relativity and guilt, confusing us more. Now I'm indifferent to the pain that provokes my understanding. I allow for it, coldly and so impersonally that it strips me – not of the actions on which I no longer count for myself, everything happens – but of an absurd passion for its materialization in the here and now. So what can I do?

a form of allowance / an exertion of force



I try to establish spaces for my gestures without constricting them, without making them conditional, keeping them alive for their small incomplete form(s) of intensity.

**Make them know me without trying to make them understand me.**

So there, a bit more free.

without reason / without possession

I know I've written of these matters in regions of language you won't understand. But I think that like those blind men, when you put your hand onto the writing, thawing it, you'll feel the unique emotion from the writing inside which I tried to simplify this agony, tried to say: what has happened here! what has happened here?

# Matter

Me too here, detained between losing it all

and going back.

This constant horror between bleeding it out

and the void.

What word can replace anguish

and not persecution.

*If they come for us*[29] I'm not there

and not here either.

I know the worst of abysses:

and in transit.

I fled from consciousness of myself

and now left divided.

That duality: to be something resembling you

and its representation.

[29] Reference to Fatimah Asghar's *If They Come for Us*

The force that pushes me too to be "a remainder"

and another woman.

Who permits me to believe myself a "self"

and other girls like us.

My holy wild daughter, the thing destroyed is not outside

and is inside the human brain.

The more effort it makes

and the more the brain can live out its myth.

As if there were truth

and it can understand.

There is only diaspora

and I hear your voice in my ear.

Your small warm hand on my breast empty of milk

and you tell me "no more."

Girls like us idle no more

and don't get anywhere.

We're beings of transit, of trajectories, of processes

and not of finality.

Night goes on falling

and between its shadows, the moon.

Like a wild animal

and makes its way home.



Moves out from behind fear

and illuminates.

Illuminates my illusion of being lost in the nothingness of my impoverished imaginary

and it can't change.

*Whereas*[30] my daughter can conceive of a more modern angle on the pain

and the plains

to make room in the mouth / for grassesgrassesgrasses.

---

[30] reference to Layli Long Soldier's *Whereas, from which "make room in the mouth / for grassesgrassesgrasees"* is taken

The doves complain as they move in circles idly no more: they come
and go.
I sit down to see how you've grown
and you look as though you were taken from the wild.
From a grassland green
and arid as its desolation.
Standing tall standing with standing rocks
and you throw your hair back to observe not the limits but the sky.
I love you in beauty I imagined
and was not.
Knowing that I won't be here later
and pass my hand over the place where another detail has grown.
I open the structure between a noun (*citizen*[31])
and its fabula (squeezing myself more tightly).
You struggle free
and move in circles against my body.

[31] references Claudia Rankine's *Citizen*

Your life devours mine

and I surrender.

Reduced again to the form of urban species that provokes no other form of ending

and resurrection.

How can we transcend this infinite black space above our heads

and move forward

before they knock on the door, wolves in sheeps' clothing,

and the planet we created collapses back.



You, ready, leap into black matter that is spatial matter

and the space is the blackness of and between your movements.

You, already, *call a wolf a wolf*[32]

and know your life's matters.

Oh, my daughter, how horrible

and possible it is here.

---

[32] references Kaveh Akbar's *Calling a Wolf a Wolf*

What does the object become without its place

and without my possession of it.

I feel horror at being so alone

and among objects.

Exploitation of all this horror

and it can't be a life!

The landscape outside eats away at me

and on the inside matters too.

I assemble a discourse (another justification)

and it's worth nothing either.

A white priest passes by in his black cassock

and causes me to lift my gaze.

There he is, as obsolete as I am,

and I go back to thinking about you.

*There is no theory of subversion that cannot also serve the cause of oppression.*
—Jacques Rancière (tr. Emiliano Battista)

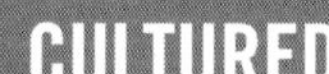
CULTURED

## Cultured

**Breathe out the old, let in the new.** I know I'm going to lose myself. The ants climb our legs and a certain change of light tells us so. The air that would come and go beneath my skirt no longer presses against our pants. In this moment, the countries beyond our country can vanish. It's just the people and me, us.

Before all thought, desire:

吐故纳新

**Sailing the seas depends on the helmsman.** We undress and enter. Knowing we'll find something, and that the boats—which seem suspended on the horizon, seem to have slipped their limits, motionless and painted there—are also ours, his. We'll swim out to them, his.

**Making our revolution** **depends on his thought:**

大海航行靠舵 手
干革命靠毛泽东思想

**A single spark can start a prairie fire.** When I met we and you met we it was still May and we were strange and different and would be for a long time after—though sometimes we shaped a sort of formless impression: something strange and indefinable divided the outline of our body from the space around us, but without making a human form and in our eyes the spark of sunlight revolved as if turned like a bicycle's spoked wheel, carried along, collecting together.

One point amid the infinite comes into view:

星星之火可以燎原

**Achieve new things for the people.** We're in geography class. We like this class. The world just barely fits in our heads. The map hangs before us with its spokes and points, Himalayas and Yangtzes.

Someone made that all up, just to make us think we belong:

为人民立新功

**The people, alone, are the motive force in the making of world history.** The beginnings of everything that seem to be reality, but isn't, because we're not outside but inside the globe, that huge globe so stubborn in its sufficiency, and even far from the classroom nothing's different: there's just the refined and cultured idea of that opaque and transparent globe that is our image of the world, always turning, imperfect and constant inside us. We like the maps and the stability of the geography that situates places in our heads. We like using graph paper to plot the latitudes and longitudes we can't measure without human inferences:

人民只有人民才是创造世界历史的动 力

**The foolish old man who moved the mountains.** We like the geography professor, the helmsman, whose eyes we must constantly avoid in order not to drown ourselves in myself. He doesn't know that while he carries on, in many ways parting the seas, I draw fish in my notebook to throw into the river:

愚翁移山

**Let a hundred flowers bloom.** Whatever one does the others all follow, watching from the corners of their irises. That's why I'm going to fold the page away from his gaze and draw a true map where he won't find me. Alone at my desk in the middle of the world I **let a hundred thoughts contend**:

白花 齐放
百家争鸣

**Seek truth from facts.** At the centre, the landscape appears and disappears. When I take the oars, you want to teach me how to row over the edge. You try to teach me: you take my hands—he's behind and above me. My fingers are lost in the middle of the boat. We try to steer but go nowhere. He explains the roundness of the earth; the sharpened tip of the compass needle, like a bicycle spoke, always precise, marking contours, lines, limits. The shadow and the truth of our body in this cultural landscape: appearance and disappearances when we try to comprehend the possible across great distances, long marches, the symmetry, forgetfulness or incarnation in other beings: animals, plants, other women. You taught us, me, all this, but I'm not a map and I hold still. I abandon myself and our selves and the dread of nearing the end:



实事求是[33]

[33] The quotes within are ancient philosophical concepts deployed by Mao, in the 1960s, during the Cultural Revolution.

*[T]he first foundational step to embracing a newfound freedom is embracing the freedom to imagine it.*

—Rinaldo Walcott

# Reproduction

**It was a beautiful Spring day**

and by now the sound of gunfire had vanished.

Where my mother was buried in Askar was a *zaatar* plant

and it seemed to be growing very straight to me.

But in fact I knew I was not a plant

and went along always with my head to the ground.

I was asked "Is it true that the nearer we come to our paroxysm of violence"

and I answered "the more we become ourselves."

Time can only tell

and only a mother who comes to the point of childbirth can tell.

## Everything which blocks the horizon

and encumbers us.

We can't see out or the smoke hasn't cleared or the dust settled

and we are safe from knowing what is coming next.

All my blood does is run headlong into life

and I know this might be to your death.

When it is someone else's pain



and I could stop it from happening.

"Wittgenstein was afraid of going mad

and that's why he became a philosopher."

I have these conversations with you

and you kick me in my ribs.

I don't remember what he'd wanted to be in the first place

and then I remember: a gardener.

**To really love things is the most complex a person can be**

and my mother had been the horizon on the sea I can no longer see.

When the funeral was over I went to the market

and bought seed packets for tomatoes, *zaatar* and radishes.

My mother was gone

and I didn't know whether to become one.

I leaned out the window as far as I liked

and I liked my heart beating faster.

Was this what it was meant to be free

and I never had to return her phone calls again.

I wondered if I could persuade my body to jump out the window

and immediately planted the seeds.

**Humans live out of curiosity**

and that's the most humane way anyway.

I was curious to see if I could harvest life



and so I tried.

There is something hypnotic about touching soil

and I could do it for hours.

I returned to the window

and looked down with a kind of resignation.

I can already see people whispering that somebody had pushed me

and saying "otherwise she wouldn't have planted the seeds."

**Autumn was on its way**

and I was mistaking thrown stones for birds.

Najiba Ahmad believes that *A bird is not a stone*

and yet I know that sometimes a bird is a stone.

Teaching philosophy in Gaza was like leaning out a window

and I knew it would not be possible for the rest of one's life.

I read in another book that Wittgenstein didn't really want to be a gardener

and actually wanted to be an aeronautical engineer.

The answers were becoming less clear

and looked down again with a kind of resignation.

**I'd made a promise to my mother to go back to the beginning**

and I've kept it.

I cannot resolve the subject or answer the question

and you bring me into a long night.

What you require of me is truth



and not imagination.

Now I am remembering and not imagining

and there is a great distance between the two.

Right now I am leaning out the window's edge

and giving birth to you there.

At the moment of supreme violence

and I can answer that I have become more ourselves.

## End Notes

### HOME

In contrast to the poems in EXILE, the companion pieces from a series called "My (Un) homelands" are meant to recount private discourse in the more personal spheres inhabited by some of the writers and artists working during these periods of war and revolution.

### EXILE

EXILE started as a series entitled "Discussions of Homelands from Memorial Park Benches" featuring revolutionary voices of great thinkers and makers regarding their destroyed former homes while seated at benches in the commemoration sites that have been built since their demolishing.



### AUDITORIUM

The poems in this series discuss language and revolution in the amphitheatres and drama theatres of collected experience, in various sites of dissent and calamity.

### MORATORIUM

Using the imperative tense, these works take discourse out of the auditoriums, the classrooms, lecture halls or public theatres and squares of the previous section, and instead allow them to take place on the ever-shifting terrains of shorelines, cemetery grounds, and wombs. *From*

*Diaspora to My Unborn Island* is a nod to the work of Terrence Hayes in *American Sonnets for my Past and Future Assassins* and *From a certain logic for dis/appearing* is a glosa dedicated to Dionne Brand and drawing from the work of Edmond Jabès.

PUBLIC

These poems began as a series called Poems of Public Record and Discourse. The translations (mine and others listed within or below) are used to create conversation between thinkers and writers at uneasy times and to show some of the process of translating previous texts as an undertaking of rethinking important concepts and philosophies. "The people want to fall, the people want the fall" features translated lines from an interview with Slavoj Žižek and Gaddafi by Hamid Dabashi in "Living In the Old World" in conversation with Hishem El-Jokh's poem "The Visa" or "التأشيرة". "A Place for Change تغيير (or Revolution)" features translated lines from Najiba Ahmad's poem "Rights + Principles" or "حقوق + مبادئ" in conversations of its translation. Measures of *Historia* features translated lines from Antón Arrufat's poem "Tempo I" in conversation with testimony from Vilma Espín's "History Will Absolve Me" or "*La historia me absolverá*" which features a Cuz line.

PRIVATE

These poem began as a series called Poems of Private Record and Diary recording more personal musings and narrations, as if notes to the self. The transgressing Arabic and English in [*Night 3*] [ضوء ٣] are not individual translations but rather different ways of continuing the same threads of thought in both languages. The haiku sections take their titles from Roland Barthes' lecture sessions on the qualities and elements that he determined to be present in Chinese and Japanese poetics.

MATTERS

Much of this material investigates land matters and matters of land on these unceded lands formerly known as North America but which should be known as many other things and in the many other ways of knowing places. The contrapuntal pieces in the series center around various forms of activism, movement, organisation. Each piece uses an iteration from a movement and also a book title from one of the many poets that included their voices in the struggles and revolutions, many of which are ongoing.



CULTURED

This series uses revolutionary slogans and also Maoist dictums from the Cultural Revolution and upends their intended meanings by contrast to real life experiences and features some of the writers known as the Misty Era poets, working in the same period with great bravery.

*Breathe out the old, let in the new* (吐故纳新 Tu gu na xin) is a four-character phrase first used by the philosopher Zhuangzi in 4th century and subsequently used by many authors including Lu Xun 鲁迅 (1881–1936), who was admired by Mao.

*Sailing the seas depends on the helmsman, making revolution depends on Mao Zedong Thought* (大海航行靠舵 手，干革命靠毛泽东思想 Dahai hangxing kao duoshou, gan geming kao Mao Zedong sixiang) is from the revolutionary song "Sailing the Seas Depends on the Helmsman", 1964, with music by Wang Shuangyin 王双印, lyrics by Li Yuwen 李郁文, edited by Zhou Enlai 周恩来. Lin Biao's calligraphic inscription of these lines, combined with the revolutionary song, made this one of the famous phrases of the Cultural Revolution. It is often found in the front pages of *Quotations from Mao Zedong* and *Newest Directives of Mao Zedong*.

*A single spark can start a prairie fire* (星星之火可以燎原 Xingxing zhi huo keyi liaoyuan; 星火燎原 Xing huo liaoyuan) is the title of an essay by Mao (1933), in *Selected Works, Vol. 1*.



*Achieve new things for the people* (为人民立新功 Wei renmin li xin gong) is the title of a small book containing two speeches by Jiang Qing, published in 1967.

*The people, and the people alone, are the motive force in the making of world history* (人民只有人民才是创造世界历史的动 力 Renmin zhi you renmin cai shi chuangzao shijie lishi de dongle) is from Mao's "On Coalition Government", in *Quotations*, ch. 11.

*The foolish old man who moved the mountains* (愚翁移山 Yu weng yi shan) is the title of an essay by Mao (1945), and one of the Three Constantly Read Articles. The story tells of an old man who set out to move two mountains, manually digging and shifting the earth. With persistence, he eventually achieved his aim.

Let a hundred flowers bloom, let a hundred thoughts contend (白花 齐放, 百家争鸣 Bai hua qifang, bai jia zhengming) is associated with Mao's quotes of the 1950s about smashing or eliminating the old and letting the past serve the present or foreign cultures serve China.

*Seek truth from the facts (*实事求是 Shí shì qiús hì) is an ancient Chinese philosophical concept. The phrase was deployed by Mao, in the 1960s, so the new leadership could reuse it and claim legitimacy toward the Cultural Revolution (文化大革命).

REPRODUCTION

The choice of biological reproduction during a time of great shelling in Gaza is considered by the speaker, who herself is a pregnant woman.

## Acknowledgments

From the time the idea of this book germinated til its completion, there have begun revolutionary passions and political disenchantments that have me now differently active and bereft. The research and the writing continues.

I am deeply grateful for the intellectual generosity of all the members and organizers and dreamers cast and recast in the process. I work from inspiration. Thank you for your archive of theoretical texts, for answering my personal questions, for militancy, for friendship, for critical eyes and patience. I am grateful for the indelible formative experiences of re-thinking the idea of tradition and making known the impossibility of the interpretation of culture.

This book began as a thesis and I was provided tranquil confidence for the potential of this project from my committee members. I was recharged to resume the solitary labors of writing from the close readings or insights given by George Abraham, Kaveh Akbar, Kazim Ali, Mirene Arsanios, Stephanie Bolster, Megan Fernandes, Ilya Kaminsky, Tess Liem, Canisia Lubrin, Katherine McKleod, Klara du Plessis, Sina Queryas, Jacob Wren, and Han Xia.

In finding its breathing, I owe thanks to Jessica Moss for my heartbeat. My sisters Erin Perry for sight and Maya Moumne for seeing. Matana Roberts for listening. Nazik Dakkach for footsteps. Farah Atoui for star dust.

Without the insistence on real work from Noemi Press, and to work better and harder, and to work through things with care and attention and humour and through error, this work would not be possible. I cannot thank Carmen, J. Michael, Diana, Ella, Sarah, Steve, and everyone at Noemi enough.

I would very much like to acknowledge and thank the lands that held me during the composition of this work and for so many days of my living. Some of the writing was done on lands that are unceded territories, some returned my blood to Cuba, some revisited China, some found love and blood in Lebanon. I owe thanks to the stewards—past, present and future that have let me swim, too, in the waters; I dream of better protection for the inhabitants of these lands and waters.

I hold the belief that emancipation is a processual right not only for humans but for every aspect of our world(s) and shared cosmos. We imagine relationally, sometimes with words and sound and sometimes with wind, with graze; how collectively we move with and because of each other.

Some parts of this book have been adapted from previously printed materials. Earlier versions of things have appeared with the Centre for Expanded Poetics, the Vallum Chapbook Series, and Gap Riot Press. Poems have been printed or prized by the *Georgia Review*, the *Capilano Review*, *Disquiet International*, *Quebec Writers' Federation*, *carte blanche*, *Moko Magazine*, *Arc Poetry Magazine*, the *Puritan*, the *Fiddlehead*, *Contemporary Verse 2*, *Journal Safar* (جورنال سفر),

*Offscreen*, a translation in *Hors Champs*, *Painted Bride Quarterly*, and more. I would like to acknowledge the support of The Social Sciences and Humanities Research Council Fellowship, The Fonds de recherche du Québec—Société et culture Fellowship, the Canada Council for the Arts, Conseil des arts et lettres du Québec towards the research and creation of this project.

I am infinitely grateful for growing up and continuing to be loved by a family suffused with a generous ethos, which always nurtures and never directs. I am sustained by the encouragement along the way. And Leticia Artola Miranda, mi abuela, I miss you.

Etel Adnan and Shahin Parhami, your words will keep wording mine. Thank you.

I have trust—that most rare and risky thing—because of my partner Radwan Ghazi Moumneh and our children Ilham Lezama and Isla Sahar and the magic of the future: mine and ours and yours.

I am looking forward to working with my sisters ahead.

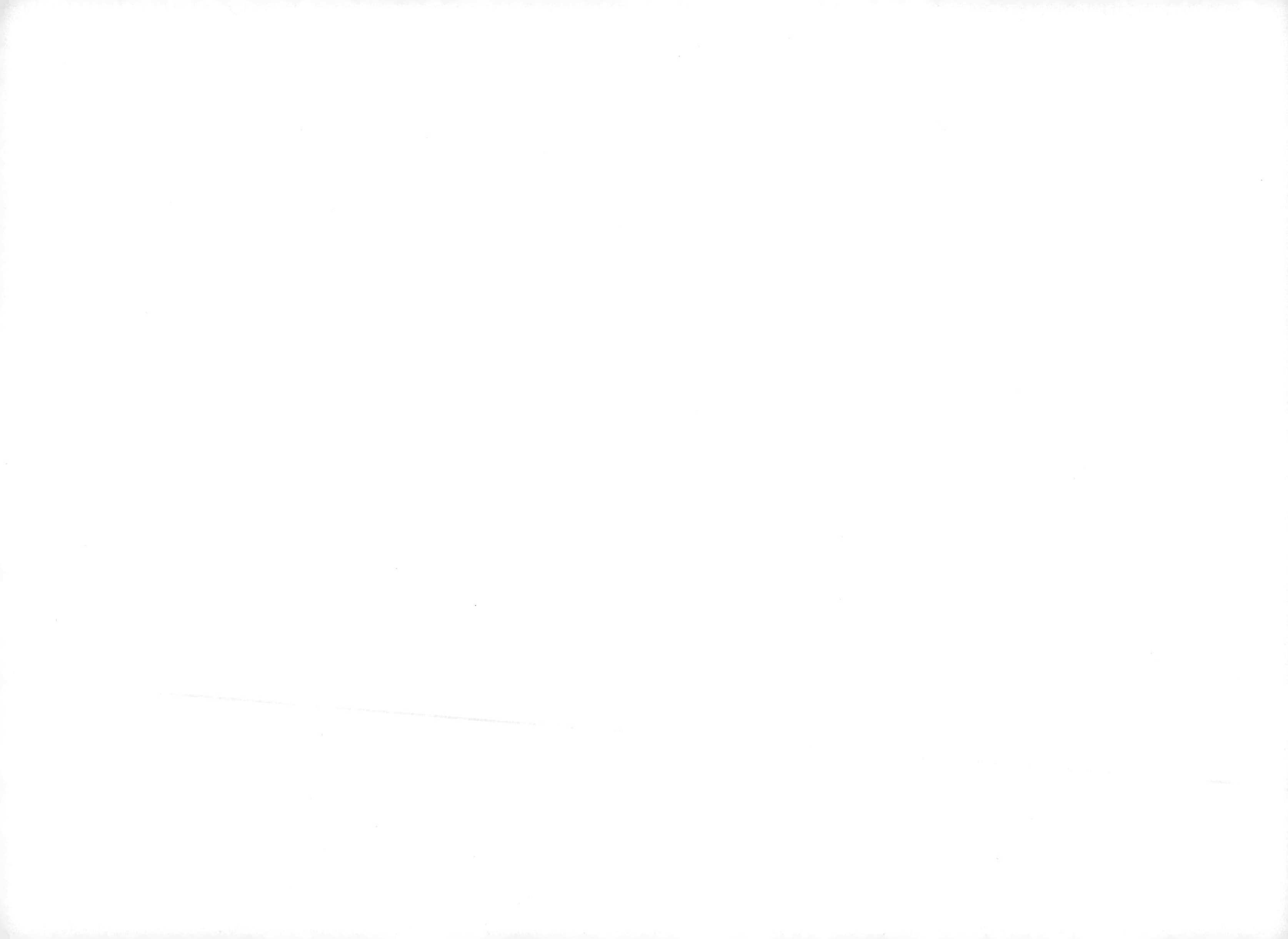